WOOD & INK

SERGEANT I/C DISCIP.

Under the peak an inch from his nose, and cricking his neck
The sergeant looked up to the sky and saw little pink spotted
frocks everywhere,
And from the little pink dolly-frocks dangled little pink legs
Some of a piggy pink, some of a pasty pink, and some more
truly pink, as pink as rose petals, and some he poked with
his pacing stick.
And under the the little pink legs were little white socks,
And under the little white socks he knew for certain were
little pink toes as soft and pink as peeled prawns,
And he longed to suck the biggest of the little pink toes and
all the others in order.
Though never printed on pink he loved the SROs as much as the
litttle pink toes and the pink spotted frocks,
But the terrible stickler's twinkle in his eye as he swigged
his pints in the mess had more to do with the little pink
toes and the tidy number ten of them.
Though the sergeant, whose name resembled eleven, would often
exceed ten at least to eleven
He drank each in order and never the sixth pint after the
seventh or the fourth pint after the fifth,
And the waxed points of his moustache would poke up as he
drank, to the ceiling if not to the sky,
To the little pink toes and the little pink feet,
And snoring after his binge he dreamt he lay under a smother
of petals and pink spotted frocks
But woke with a shout in a terrible sweat whenever an untidy
tangle threatened to strangle him,
And never before reveille could he sleep again, no not even a wink.

Alan Dixon

SGT.
ELVIN

WOOD & INK

Wayne Burrows
Alan Dixon
Paul McLoughlin
Helena Nelson
Andrew Sant
Jo Shapcott
John Hartley Williams

Shoestring Press

Printed by imprintdigital
Upton Pyne, Exeter
www.imprintdigital.net

Typeset by types of light
typesoflight@gmail.com

Published by Shoestring Press
19 Devonshire Avenue, Beeston, Nottingham, NG9 1BS
(0115) 925 1827
www.shoestringpress.co.uk

First published 2013

ISBN 978 1 907356 88 9

FOREWORD

In 2011 Shoestring Press published *73 Woodcuts* by the poet and artist, Alan Dixon. I had long been an admirer of Dixon's poetry and in 2005 was delighted to publish his collection *The Ogling of Lady Luck*. The book had as a cover image a striking woodcut made by the author, and over the years, as I saw more of these, I became convinced that they deserved to reach as wide an audience as possible. This view was shared by the poet Helena Nelson, who used several of Alan's images for her own Happen*Stance* Press, and also by the poet Andrew Sant. With their encouragement I saw through the press *73 Woodcuts*, one of the handsomest books Shoestring has published. And that, I thought, as I held the book in my hands, would be that.

But then Andrew sent me a sequence of poems he had derived from Alan's images, poems that between them made up a witty, affectionate, and acutely observant narrative, though they weren't, thank goodness, intended as verbal equivalents of Alan's woodcuts. Instead, the woodcuts provided the trigger to fire the poet's own imagination. It occurred to me that other poets whom I knew to be admirers of Alan's work might in like spirit want to try their hands at providing poems to place beside or against individual woodcuts. Invitations went out and the result is *Wood & Ink*, a book the press is delighted and proud to be able to publish.

John Lucas

CONTENTS

WAYNE BURROWS

ZEHRA

It's this white clip, firmly slotted into a night of hair,
that makes her profile luminous, her brow a shore
against a sea of dark. It's the fish-tail curl
bridging cheekbone and jowl like a folded wing,
a hint of exhaustion that cups each eye,
the pinch at one corner of her downturned mouth
that defines this girl, maps thought in her face,
has me imagining I might have known her once.

But it's the way she's pressed into this paper's grain
like light inverted against a black plank,
a stranger waking aboard a late-evening train
when a tannoy crackles and doors let in the winter cold,
that moment when we both stand up to leave,
gather our bags from the luggage racks,
let our eyes meet, lock and unlock, completely blank,
that tells me who she was is no business of mine.

SELF

These serrations at my jaw-line, the jagged edges of my closed mouth,
my eyes like barbs on a barbed wire fence, my blunt knife's nose
against the insistent gouge of a cityscape where I appear almost at ease.
Do you know already who I am? Or do I still need to spell it out?

INQUISITORS

His eyes seem turned both ways at once.
His colleague expounds on innocence.

His ear exaggerates its presence here.
A tab's turned outward but doesn't hear.

His head is round as a hard-boiled egg.
He thinks everyone is trying to pull his leg.

His moustache and shirt are both pitch black.
He fears what's said behind his back.

NOCTURNE

My head is a matchstick, burnt out,
bent forward in the black wind
that sharpens the prow
of a black boat on black water
where moonlight gleams.
I have lit the candles
in a mourning room
and left them burning,
each twisted to fit its metal sconce
like a root-stock pressed
into sodden ground.
Now these currents
draw my boat downstream.
There is no oar, no rudder,
no way to steer or change my course,
only the journey,
this cold breeze off the bright waves,
my own hands
hanging dry at my sides
in a black boat cut adrift at night.

HEADS

The cabaret opens with a white goat in a cardboard dress
bleating against a bare stage to an audience of two.
Both drink neat gin, take hashish with tinctures of opium,
stamp themselves against a white wall like the Chinese for 'twins'.
A Swiss flag droops behind the optics above the bar.
Edelweiss are shrouded in blue cigarette smoke
like lights in a nebula that won't be seen for a century more.
The curtains are green. A barman wipes glasses with a red towel.
Smoke and gunfire rumble over the mountainsides
where wild flowers seem undisturbed and the air is still.
There are striped tablecloths. The goat goes on,
bleating, chewing at the cardboard collar of its painted dress.
Something might be taking shape in these heads
but hasn't formed. Even they don't yet know what it is.

PROCESSION

The witch, the boy, the dog and the geese
went out in the darkness as bold as you please;
walked too quickly, walked too slow,
walked onwards always heel to toe.

The dog, the witch, the geese and the boy
went into the woods without knowing the way;
strode over cinders, strode over stones,
couldn't tell which way led home.

The boy, the geese, the witch and the dog
saw juicy red berries on a green bush by a log;
they hadn't eaten, they hadn't fed,
tried a berry and fell down dead.

The geese, the dog, the boy and the witch
were covered with leaves in a deep brown ditch;
nobody missed them, nobody knew
where it was they'd meant to go.

COMPLICATED FIGURE

I am disassembled. My broken body's machine
is a puzzle of undone hooks and lines nothing solves.
I turn against cities and firework sparks,
blur stars with darkness, torsos with faces, let legs be arms
and every part of me interchanged
where nothing's fixed bar the outer frame.
I disembody myself, limb by limb, angle by angle
and bone by bone, to this unruly clutter of building blocks,
the coming disorder made plain in my form
as a neon sign's flash or lighthouse beam
slice their words and bright arcs through a thick fog.
What next? Do I reassemble or disperse in space?
Become a cog in someone else's paradise
or a swastika? Do you even suppose there's a difference?

Paul McLoughlin

BALLOON OVER THE CITY

Avenues of bricked-in scrapers
list toward a floating ambulance,
the anxious young traipsing
their hair and make-up home
or out or away, one sawn-off
head with teacup-handle ears
and ink-stained pate impossible
to read cannot phalanx past
the neck-craned girl quickly
enough. It is like this every
day. The light appals. Only
the crossed balloon can breathe.

IN A SPIN

She's in a hula-hoop, in charge
of whatever treadmill's been
devised, her polka-dotted apron
wide-eyed and open-mouthed
and fancy-free, her dainty,
fish-eyed platforms leaving
go-faster stripes scratched
in her wake. She fits exactly
as if she's by her den expressed,
fingers blunted tines that
gently stretch the rolling
as she grows, a gathering
ball of string preparing to be
set aside for further use.

HOMAGE TO MALEVICH

The weightless, murderous man
runs from himself, red-faced,
blue-robed, white-trimmed,
past an arrow pointing back
to where he's been, his medal
pinned in its decorated place.

A brace of birds on a mission
fly from sword to crucifixion-
sword across a sky blood-red
from burning fields, to recce
pipe-cleaner limbs floating over
autumn leaves, the long-legged
lightness of a tyrant's mid-air
tread, the whippy bend of knees.

A coat-hanger puppy paddles
over familiar, altered ground
to keep up, the best he can do
to demonstrate his readiness.

 Homage to Malevich (164 x 115)

HOMMAGE TO
MALEVICH

COMPANIONS

The gnarled tree's a hardy
laurel sad to see them go,
this pair of baggy-trousered
companions in a rootless
universe with the tall hat
and flat cap they swap
religiously to pass the time,
the too-tight boots, the stick
the one who needs it has to
bend to lean on, a stoop
the other tells him will be
permanent. This together-
ness may eventually
get them down, but they've
a way to go before they lose
the spring in their step,
the will to blame each other
for the mess they're in.

AD

CAPTAIN M'NURE

> CAPITAINE BORDURE: *costume de musicien hongrois tres collant rouge. Grand manteau, grand epée, bottes crénelées, tchapska à plumes*
>
> (Alfred Jarry, *Ubu roi*)

Look, you can't control what's done to you—
in the choppy English Channel (aka *La Manche*)
even my name slips off the edge of heraldry
into that fertiliser Alf would call a pile of shit.
I play piano in his sticky red, (or 'skin-tight red',
depending on your preference, or dictionary).
What I think is neither here nor there. The
skull my tchapska sports is variously judge
or snowman for no good reason I can fathom.
Inside my head I'm sane. I have to be
as I'm imagined, wear moustache and
buttoned uniform, depress discordant keys
while you deceive yourselves. Watching
lips move is how you learned to smile.

Not before time, I can tell you, Kodaly's busy
teaching Hungary to locate Glover's moving
middle C, follow his hands and sing. It will be
more than enough eventually to launch a van
with loudspeakers, a thousand tanks and talk
of crushing victory, but enjoy it while it lasts.
I'm a response to crazy, not a crazy work of art.
I go away but some unsettled soul will always
haul me back.

CAPT.
McNURE
AD

DANCER

Bundle of muscle, hair
flowing in the no-breeze
of her studio, joints aflex
in well-oiled armour, lost
in the sweat of movement,
as if the clank of grace, of
innocence is audible where
juices rise, the passion
of the dance. There is
a modern world outside,
barred and curtainless,
that hasn't caught her yet.

HOLDING ON

She's stretched, her hair
loosely horizontal like
so many telegraph wires
a bird keeps pace with
with a view to resting on one
when the fancy takes it,
her hands gripping horn
and tail, breasts and legs
pulled shamelessly apart.
The beast aroused speeds
up but she is used to that.
It's what they do, these
unicorns. She also knows
eventually she'll come
to rest exhilarated.

NUDE ON A SOFA

He's pleased with himself.
He knows his time will come,
and later at the opening
he'll call the body holy.
I smile because there's little
point in beating myself up.
I'll leave that to the likes of him.
Who knows if I'll become regarded
as a muse of some significance.
Can you see me painting him?

Helena Nelson

THE AESTHETES

So what if we *are* effete?
Better languor
than anger.
Though not athletic types
behold the old school tie.

You sport the spotted,
beautifully knotted
as befits the élite,
and even I
bear stripes.

AD

DREAM

I am advancing but my paws do not touch the ground—
not quite—I am lighter than the scent of an early frost
and my fur is streaming behind me and it is spring
and butterflies are all around. And now one of the host
is about to alight on my unhackled spine, and I know
not through my nose but in my blood
that we are one. We are of the essence.
We are almost ineffably good.

THE MERMAID'S VIEW

Landmaids will mythologize:
beauty is overrated.
We are not obsessed with size.
We are understated.
We do not have to wear bras
and baldness is rare.
Luring sailors onto rocks is, of course,
brutal. We do not care,
we do it while singing
goodbye, goodbye, goodbye
because it is in our genes, like bringing
certain types of octopi
home as pets. We do not have vets.
We do not have shops.
We have fierce mermen. We try
to resist them but it is no use.
In the main we choose
to lose our maidenhoods.
It gets
darker, rougher, the wind slaps
to and fro and floods
our heads with thoughts of getting away
but we melt into spray.

NECESSITY

Through rain or snow
with stooping head
and spirits low,
man walks dog:
whatever the weather
he must go.

Andrew Sant

PIGEONS

Three pigeons: one preening,
one watching, another, over the rooftops,
flying – each styliferous
as a hieroglyph. Nearby are shops.

That's obvious in my loose reading
of the situation: pigeons flock
in urban spaces other
avian species shun, prefer a block

of rundown flats, no shortage,
to remainder forest. Your affection
for these birds, Alan, is also clear.
But where are their nests?

Never mind. The design
of the woodcut is fine without one.
Perhaps next time pigeons have the freedom
of your head you'll chisel some.

Meantime, these birds are always close,
adapted to scraps, a favourite, quiche
untested by those threatened species
trapped in an ecological niche.

 Pigeons (94 x 120)

TWO CATS

East Sussex cats, local,
are perhaps the inspiration,
subject to the influence
of German Expressionism.
They look alarmed. I know
you like these creatures, Alan,
in concord with your wife.
These two mousers
look as if they might have chased
the pair of you out
of the house. They remind
me that I'm not so keen –
which is not to say I don't stroke them –
wouldn't keep one, unlike
my neighbours who have three hunters.
Hereabouts, your antipodean critic
is the native species
rescue service: skinks,
gheckos, the small long-snouted
antechinus, an endemic rat.
There's no place for any of them
in the mouth of a cat.
That you've made other woodcuts
of the species we plundering humans
butter-up, proves, admirably,
your own attachment.
There's not, I know, so much left
to catch in England. Here, on my wall,
among other woodcuts by you,
there's one more predacious culprit
framed. I love it above them all.

 Two Cats (128 x 68)

TRAMPS IN RAIN/TRAMPS IN SNOW

Tramps in snow, tramps in rain,
I recall others – Alan,

what draws you to depict
these guys? An empathy

perhaps for their gaining
from what on foot they lack.

No car. No phone. The same
position as your own.

I admire this as much
as the engaging woodcuts. No slaves,

these roamers, to consumption
or convention, except

each has obtained a hat
in each composition.

No women tramps, I see,
at large in skilfully

chiselled weather – way beyond
the pejorative hurt contained

in the word. So be it.
Women are better off portrayed

elsewhere in the work, naked.
Diagonal rain, those incised lines,

the two tramps make through
as surely reminds me

of the day we got soaked
walking high along the coast

as that, in any context,
the appreciation

of art is never pure –
and now I can also see

through the brisk memory
of clifftop weather, these

lines, parallel, contain in part
a sample portrait

of the artist via his art,
a walker, unperturbed

by rain blown horizontal;
stoical northerner,

hoarder of found objects,
the wood for woodcuts never

bought – scavenged, aptly,
for the homages to tramps.

WOMAN WITH EARRINGS

The woman was spotted on a bus
if I remember what I heard correctly – an individual
not, as in other woodcuts, archetype.

It's black and white, she's young
not old: there's not a black
line on her white face. The earrings

perhaps declare Eastbourne style.
Call it maritime gothic. The head's in profile.
This reveals where in relation to her

the artist sat, his eye not on the traffic.
My copy of the edition of eight
is number four, initialled, and inscribed

"For Andrew", which places me specifically
in this general picture – and elsewhere on a bus,
several times, sitting next to Alan Dixon.

NOCTURNE

A theft during a still, moonless night –
then later next day a headline
in the *Evening Standard*
PAINTING STOLEN FROM THE TATE

This fantasy names the work
as 'The Sea B', a brooding night seascape
by Emil Nolde. In its place
the two cunning art thieves have left
a clue to their identities,
a questionably droll riposte
printed in black ink: AA

These guys value the work
more than do the general public.
That's their excuse. Meantime,
while the police pursue their lame enquiries
and the painting rockets into notoriety,
'The Sea B' is safely hanging
in the garage where a woodcut
titled 'Nocturne', among many others,
was created. Perhaps a cop
up to the job might discern the pleasing
influence of Emil Nolde.

The garage doors are open,
this is how the artist likes it
while he applies his weight
to block and paper, owns
no press – nor needs the interest
of his neighbours, fortunate,
since as he reports they display none
which is why, for all to see,
the now notorious painting is safe.

Should this indifference change, amazingly,
a little fame beam like a steady headlight
into the garage that never sees a car
or some grass recalls that I once said, darkly,

I covet 'The Sea B'
more than any other painting in the Tate
(which is not to say I wouldn't
share it with a mate) and then link
ink to black ink of which
in the garage there's plenty,
the two As will surely be as nimble
at returning as in nicking
from the public gaze
the now famous painting – and, hey,
now that it is they'll return it anyway.

HEADS

Alan Dixon: poet, painter, amateur
ornithologist, grower, expands the list
of his pursuits – the busyness
of several heads under a single hat.

A feature of his woodcuts:
heads together. In the group
I'm studying I detect, at a guess,
the influence of 20th century primitivism.

We all have many faces; it's unifying them
that is tricky. What does the publisher
who asked for these pieces dream
of receiving from a problematic me?

I have a part to play, a role,
which I make up as I proceed, influenced
by the life and work (my gathered
knowledge) of a manifold man.

Will both publisher and subject
forgive any mischief, the connecting tissue?
They both know me. So, reader,
risking poems that are hardly ekphrastic

(I know my limits) they serially stretch
into something somewhat elastic.

 Heads (101 x 99)

LEX BANNING

Today it's hot here, Alan,
cold there, I imagine,

unremarkably so, except
there in East Sussex

you keep warm on frosty
mornings a knowledge

of Australian art
and poetry rare

in any climate –
where, in yours,

you likely spotted, like an exotic
bird in a winter tree,

a remarkable copy in that
godsend, Camilla's Bookshop –

its popular parrot in a cage
I surmise will never stray –

of the Angus and Robertson
There was a Crooked Man collection,

and freed the poems
of a man never free

of his physical affliction
from the patient rows and rows

of books, all second-hand. Hence
the cheerful portrait of Lex Banning.

LEX B
AD

APPLE PICKERS

I can't decide for this take
of the requested ten
which woodcut, one of plenty,

to penultimately select.
"Sisyphus" would misrepresent
the dilemma and "In a Spin" extend it.

I'm tempted by a group
of expressionist human heads, indebted
to how subjective one can get,

like being a guest bedazzled
by a lavish banquet. But I need
a tramp's eye for a single tasty pie.

Another tramp? Or better – yes! – select
the convictive apple (not ripe hop or pear
or berry) pickers, prominent

among the other works I also prize.

LATE FOR BREAKFAST

The wife can't see her bearded,
hopeful husband is about to enter
the room in which she sits, and he
can't see the decades of rage

etched upon his spouse's face.
This is a dramatic moment – one frame
in a long, domestic narrative.
The teapot, presumably, is no longer hot.

I've chosen to conclude, decisively,
with this striking woodcut; bet it in no way
reflects events in the harmonious
Dixon household where, in my times

as a guest, breakfast exposes
no source of friction – and, if I may, suggest
what happens next: the husband begs,
the wife plugs his gob with a hard-boiled egg.

Jo Shapcott and John Hartley Williams

MAN, DOG AND MOON

Dick W's cat was actually a fox.
It had a tail of knives and a chisel nose
and a string of beads where its legs should be.
The fox can hear everything you say.
As you read this poem, gaze on this picture
then break into a run, clutching your pole
like Dick, who had never seen a real cat.
Those Chelsea boots he bought in Chelsea
and the waistcoat he didn't buy in Waistcote
and the Tyrolean hat he stole from Onkel Franz
were his setting-out-on-a-quest costume.
He knew when an illuminated **D** in the sky
appeared, it was time. He called his cat
(which was actually a fox), pulled on
his Christmas Tree jacket, put lamps
on his knees and aimed his beard at the North.

AD

TRAMPS IN RAIN

This is more than rain, it's rain plus.
It's that lascivious white woman in the sky
pulling the water down from black clouds
that stretch to the moon. And I'm thinking
Why can't I look at her? Why can't Bill
allow me to raise my eyes? The law says:
Eyes front! Hats low! Collars up! –
meanwhile the white woman sends
oversexed squirrels to attack us. Bill says
They're only trees! but Oh boy! do I feel
woeful. Rain closes our eyes, fills up our
brain-pans, and I can feel the squirrels
squirming up my trouser-leg, but I keep
squelching along, dreaming of better.
Bill says *Trees!* again. He's going mad.
He wants to go horizontal to
head-butt the thick rain stripes.
Then a white river rises in a column
and our hats suck up maps of the weather –
and so we plod on like England
dreaming of elephants, emperors, anything…

SKELETAL DOG WALKER

The dead dog-walker steps out
with his pack. His dogs are eager
to eat other dogs they meet on the way.
Poodles are best. That poodle-high
lasts all morning. Grunter, the lead dog,
slips Dachshunds down his throat –
from squeal to final tail-wag a joy.
The dead dog-walker keeps order
barking spectral commands. His
oversized clogs hide invisible
feet, good for kicking spaniels.
His pockets fill up with poop-bags:
When they are heavy enough
he trades the contents for
the sacred *merde* of giant Rottweilers
which he uses for mandible conditioner
and knuckle cream. Do not
approach him. The words he speaks
are lethal. His breath is a turd breeze.
Under his mac there only graves.

BATHERS AND GULLS

I was born in a duckpond
wearing a white sheet. They kept
switching the lighthouse off
to fool me. Octopuses nudged me.
I grew an arm and four fingers.
I aimed my mental powers at heaven.
Seagulls were sent to teach me
a lesson in splashing.
I grew an ocean.

Life goes fast when you shout
for help. Not so much drowning
as yelping, I grew a long-distance
swimmer in a black cap, towing
a squid behind her, a giant sea-
urchin, and fronds of lacy splurge.
My work was finished when I saw
a pale, amniotic, inspirational, electric
seagull posing on a diving board.
I became the ghost of lobsters past.

LOOKING BACK

I am the Prince of Playing cards.
A joker is stuck to my chest
and the juju figure of my old Mum
dances with glee at the whiskery cat
who wants to eat my coat.
Why is my head on back to front?
My friend, have you never played poker?
The moon adores my face and
strokes my T-square nose. I'm
fooling the moon with a feral cat.
Observe my saw teeth hands.
My neck is blunt as an axe.
I spit little space ships at cities and
trump the sky by leaving by coming
and shuffle your diamonds to dust.

DANTE AND VIRGIL

Our ghoul-mother was horrified
when she saw us creep out of the womb.
She gave my brother to a team
of doctors who put his face in a cage.
Rats chewed him down to a wink.

Don't we look earnest? My brother's
haircut is sharp-whittled pine sticks.
I have a floppy cut, barbed-wire and
death-cord. My dream is a skeleton
rattling for joy as it does the Yahoo Leap.

Truth is: that's an X-ray taken last Fall
after the Bomb Test went terribly wrong
and we all became bundles of skippity
bones. We're in one of those booths
where they take your photo and laugh.

TOGETHER

I was tunnelling my way into
the bank with my nuclear
drill and laser helmet
when I became aware of shrill cries
from the rest of the gang behind.

Oscar Spoonhead and Peeping Bob
had formed themselves into
a human drill-bit with me at the head!
I whirled into the flinty brick,
sparks flew from my nose and ears,
cacophonous shrapnel bulleted past –
we broke through! Breathing stale
bank air was boring after ducking grit
but I could smell the money and we
were hungry! I pointed my forehead
at the safe and liberated floods
of newly fashioned Euro-mints. Oscar
and Peeping Bob were dynamite
and blew the goodies into sacks.
We ate ourselves daft that night.

Wayne Burrows

THE CHANCELLOR'S SONG

(after Alfred Jarry: *Ubu Cuckolded*, Act 2, Scene 5)

Tremble in fear at the Great Lord of Finance,
this over-privileged shit who still fills his pants!

Too late to shout when he skins your arse
or chucks your neck under his henchman's axe.

He looks at the world through half-moon specs,
uptight as a man who's never had any sex.

Come dawn he'll rise from his brown leather chair
then go outside and foul the morning air.

He'll slam the door open, drag his soft rear about
like a rat in a larder when the lights go out,

for every day he's got so many visits to make
and every visit causes somebody somewhere to quake!

He's pricked up his ears! He's kicking a bum!
He's out on the balcony! He's banging a drum!

He's giving law-makers their god-awful papers
and with a flailing kick and his pointed stick,

a crust and raw onion to keep them from hunger,
he's sending them off to vent his anger!

Then it's straight back indoors with himself
to check the cuckoo clock on his mantel-shelf:

"Great Christ, it's six", he roars. "We're running late".
With that he whacks his lady wife's bald pate

and from his gob blows a fart of stale breezes:
"Fetch my shit-brush and my sharpest cash-tweezers!"

"Dear Ubu, permit your good wife one suggestion:
try washing your face. Is there any other option?"

But Ubu's refusal's both unreasoned and firm:
he's not slaughtered his way past the rank and infirm

to end up taking his orders from her! Lord of Finance!
King of Aragon, Poland and (sometimes) France!

He'll thread filthy britches with overstretched braces
and do as he pleases without washing off faeces.

Outside's a world blasted by wind, rain and snow.
He turns his pink buttocks to the landscape below.

LA CHANSON DU DÉCERVELAGE

(after Alfred Jarry: *Ubu Cuckolded*, Act 3, Scene 3)

I was a cabinet maker and I lived in the town
by the shadow of All Saints, a church of renown.
My wife was a milliner like so many girls
and every month we could settle our bills.
We lacked for nothing, made the best of life:
I'd knock up some cupboards, then my humble wife.
But whenever a Sunday promised no cloud
we'd put on our finery and head down the road.

We'd watch the Debrainer's polished screws
gunge the cogs that drove them with human glue!
Watch Rentiers tremble! Skulls drilled through!
Roar: Hooray for Horny Ass! Vive Père Ubu!

Our two little darlings were all smeared with jam,
we wiped both with a tissue, put one in a pram.
We bundled them onto the back seat of the car
and merrily drove off towards the Square.
When we got there the crowds rushed at the gate
and you wouldn't get in if you turned up late.
There were fights and stabbings for front row spots.
I stood on a stone to keep my shoes clear of guts.

We'd watch the Debrainer's polished screws
gunge the cogs that drove them with human glue!
Watch Rentiers tremble! Skulls drilled through!
Roar: Hooray for Horny Ass! Vive Père Ubu!

Soon my wife and I are both sprayed with blood,
our brats in brains, so it's really getting good.
We're all singing, stamping and ready to shout
whenever the Paladin pulls a new blade out!
We're not more than halfway through the fair
when I spot an old bastard I owe a thick ear.
So I yell at him: "Oi! You standing there one row back!
You robbed me once! I'll break your neck!"

We'd watch the Debrainer's polished screws
gunge the cogs that drove them with human glue!
Watch Rentiers tremble! Skulls drilled through!
Roar: Hooray for Horny Ass! Vive Père Ubu!

Then I felt the familiar rough hands of *ma famme*
take hold of my trousers and threaten my ham.
In the confusion she hands me a bag of fresh shit,
says: "I want entertainment and this isn't it!"
And in that instant, while the Paladin's back is turned,
I grab dung and take aim with my own best hand.
Egged on by my wife's hardly eloquent words
I shower bastard *and* Paladin in a hail of brown turds.

We'd watch the Debrainer's polished screws
gunge the cogs that drove them with human glue!
Watch Rentiers tremble! Skulls drilled through!
Roar: Hooray for Horny Ass! Vive Père Ubu!

All at once the crowd jeered and I almost escaped
but too many grabbed at me, blood-fuelled and enraged.
I found my body submitted to the public vote
when their boots kicked my bollocks up into my throat.
They mashed all the blood and guts I contained
through a hole barely big enough to crack an egg in.
But that's the thing with Debrainings and thinning out ranks.
You'll turn up like a Lord then go home on a plank.

We'd watch the Debrainer's polished screws
gunge the cogs that drove them with human glue!
Watch Rentiers tremble! Skulls drilled through!
Roar: Hooray for Horny Ass! Vive Père Ubu!